Visualizing The Parables

Five Short Dramas For Worship

Lynn Robert Schlessman

CSS Publishing Company, Inc., Lima, Ohio

VISUALIZING THE PARABLES

Copyright © 2004 by
CSS Publishing Company, Inc.
Lima, Ohio

The original purchaser may photocopy material in this publication for use as it was intended (i.e., worship material for worship use; educational material for classroom use; dramatic material for staging or production). No additional permission is required from the publisher for such copying by the original purchaser only. Inquiries should be addressed to: Permissions, CSS Publishing Company, Inc., P.O. Box 4503, Lima, Ohio 45802-4503.

Scripture quotations are from the *New Revised Standard Version of the Bible*, copyright 1989 by the Division of Christian Education of the National Council of the Churches of Christ in the USA. Used by permission.

For more information about CSS Publishing Company resources, visit our website at www.csspub.com or e-mail us at custserv@csspub.com or call (800) 241-4056.

ISBN 0-7880-1950-3   PRINTED IN U.S.A.

*I dedicate these plays to my wife Sue,
who has been reading and hearing
most everything I have written
for the past 32 years
and most always
says a kind and gracious word.*

Table Of Contents

Foreword	7
1. The Ten Bridesmaids *(Based on Matthew 25:1-12)*	9
2. The Prodigal Son *(Based on Luke 15:11-32)*	17
3. The Good Samaritan *(Based on Luke 10:25-37)*	25
4. The Rich Man *(Based on Mark 10:17-27)*	31
5. The Great Banquet *(Based on Luke 14:16-24)*	37

Foreword

My goal in writing these plays was to give people some new ways to think about these familiar stories while involving lots of people in the action. While the interpretations are not original (I used Robert Farrar Capon and Bernard Brandon Scott's *Hear Then The Parable* and some other resources for ideas), most of the plays move in directions that many churchgoers might not expect. Most of all, I hoped the congregation would think about Jesus as one who meets them where they are.

In the performances I directed, the actors ranged from junior high students to retirees. Everyone read his/her lines from a manuscript. The Bible-time characters were dressed in Bible-time outfits and the modern-day folks dressed the way modern folks do.

The movement and changes of scene that are used in a production will depend on the space where the play is performed. My advice is to move all around the space you have available — the more movement and change of location the better.

There are a number of names and locations that fit my congregation. These will need to be changed to fit your local sports teams, restaurants, and so on.

I wrote these plays for a worship setting, though I think they might be even more effective in the classroom or opening devotions for a church council or a congregational meeting. A retreat using any one or all five plays might be fun.

I enjoyed writing and directing these plays. I hope you will find them helpful.

1. The Ten Bridesmaids

(Based on Matthew 25:1-12)

Characters
Bill
Fred
Foolish 1-5 (five people)
Wise 1-5 (five people)
Bridegroom

(Phone rings)

Bill: Hello. Oh, hi! I've been meaning to talk with you. But can I put you on hold for a moment? There is something I need to be taking care of right now. I'll be right back to you.

Fred: *(Enters from behind altar)* Hi, Bill. What are you up to?

Bill: Nothing much. Just checking the *TV Guide* to see if there is a good movie on tonight.

Fred: I've given up on that. It's just easier to rent one — fits my schedule.

Bill: I know what you mean. There is nothing worse than having a night at home and seeing that the only movies being shown have two stars.

Fred: Or I've already seen them.

Bill: Twice.

(Phone beeps)

Fred: What's that?

Bill: Just my phone. Someone is on hold. It beeps to remind me.

Fred: Well, shouldn't you answer it?

Bill: I'll get to it in a moment. There is plenty of time.

Fred: Whatever.

Bill: Say, did you see that there is that new Perkins restaurant up at the intersection of 90 and 83?

Fred: Yeah, it sure went up fast. One day there was nothing there — seems like the next time I drove by they were open for business.

Bill: Have you ever eaten at a Perkins?

Fred: Yeah.

Bill: What sort of a restaurant is it?

Fred: Sort of a cross between Bob Evans and Baker's Square.

Bill: You mean great for older folks who aren't worrying about their cholesterol?

Fred: Exactly!

(Phone beeps again)

Fred: Don't you think you should take that guy off hold?

Bill: Oh, I've done this before. He'll be waiting. Say, did you see the *Plain Dealer* today? Looks like the Indians may not be so bad after all. If Omar Vizquel can just have a good season they may win the division.

Fred: I'm not so sure. All my life I have believed in the Indians in the spring. Come June we will have a clearer picture.

Bill: That may be, but I am glad the season is almost here. With the way the Cavs have been, it will be good to have something to care about again. Life is so boring without a good team to follow.

Fred: I know what you mean. When the Indians are winning they give me a daily dose of excitement. These winter days seem awfully gray without a team to follow.

(Phone beeps again)

Fred: Why don't you answer that thing so we do not have to listen to the beeping?

Bill: No, as soon as I answer it I will be tied up. I've heard from him before — he won't be satisfied with just a few minutes.

Fred: Then hang up on him.

Bill: Oh, I wouldn't want to do to that. That would be really dumb.

Fred: Really dumb — who is it on the phone?

Bill: Jesus.

Fred: Jesus?

Bill: Jesus. You know, the one who loves me more than he loves his own life. Jesus who gave his life for me. Jesus who has prepared a place for me. He calls — I put him on hold. I'll find some time to talk with him later when I'm not so busy.

Fred: Did you ever hear the story about the ten bridesmaids?

Bill: No. I don't think I've heard that one.

Fred: Let me tell it to you. *(Reads Matthew 25:1-5 as the bridesmaids enter)*

Foolish 1: Isn't it great that we were invited to the party?

Wise 1: I hear there is going to be a great band.

Foolish 2: And marvelous food.

Wise 2: Everyone who is anyone will be there.

Foolish 3: I heard that there is just going to be no end to this party.

Wise 3: I am sure glad I was invited.

Foolish 4: Say, what's in the flask?

Wise 4: Extra oil in case the bridegroom is late.

Foolish 5: Don't worry, he's taking care of everything. All we have to do is show up.

Wise 5: You never know how long into the night we will wait. It can take a lot of oil during a long, dark night.

Foolish 4: Say, it is getting kind of late. I think I will get a little rest before the big event.

Wise 4: Sounds like a good idea to me.

Foolish 4: I wonder why he is taking so long.

Wise 3: He'll be here soon, I know it.

Wise 2: Sure glad I brought some extra oil.

(Bridesmaids talk about it getting late, drift off to sleep one by one)

Fred: *(Reads verse 6)* But at midnight there was a shout, "Look! Here is the bridegroom! Come out to meet him."

(Phone beep wakes them)

Wise 5: What was that? Is it time?

Foolish 5: Time for the party.

Wise 1: My lamp is almost out. I'm sure glad I brought extra oil.

Foolish 2: Give us some of your oil, for our lamps are going out.

Wise 3: No, there will not be enough for you and for us; you had better go to the dealers and buy some for yourselves.

Foolish 4: Please, can you give me some oil?

Wise 1: If I share with you I won't have enough for myself. You better head for the store to buy some.

(While the following is being read, the bridegroom and the wise bridesmaids process down the center aisle to an area where they will be sharing the wedding feast)

Fred: *(Reads verse 10)* And while they went to buy it, the bridegroom came, and those who were ready went with him into the wedding banquet; and the door was shut. Later the other bridesmaids came also saying:

Foolish 4: Lord, Lord, open to us!

Bridegroom: Truly I tell you, I do not know you.

(Foolish bridesmaids walk off dejectedly)

Bill: What kind of story is that? What happened to sharing and mercy and forgiveness? I learned all about Jesus in confirmation — I say, "I'm sorry," and Jesus says, "Don't worry — I'll take care of things for you."

Fred: Jesus is the one who told this story. He must have had a reason.

Bill: Are we supposed to believe in grace or not? This story makes it sound as if we need to earn our salvation — dragging some heavy oil container through life. I have always been taught to trust that Jesus will save me. The foolish thought the Lord would take care of things for them, but he treats them like they were strangers.

Fred: Maybe they had been treating him as if he did not mean much to them.

Bill: What are we supposed to do, become monks and make vows of chastity and obedience and poverty? I can't believe this.

(Phone beeps again)

Fred: All of those bridesmaids were invited to the party. They were in. But maybe the foolish were putting Jesus on hold — "Jesus, oh, I'll get to you later ... Jesus, no time for you now ... Jesus I'm busy with so many things." They kept him on hold so long that by the time they got to the party they didn't know Jesus and he didn't know them.

Bill: Well, what is that oil all about? What is it that keeps the light burning through the long, dark night?

Fred: I think of the light as faith in Jesus. The darkness comes to both the foolish and the wise. But the foolish think they can handle the darkness on their own, that there will always be enough oil to keep the light of faith burning. But there is so much darkness — so much disappointment, so much sadness, so much pain.

Bill: And the wise know that faith must be fed with God's word, and the Lord's Supper. And praying, and gathering with other Christians. Otherwise the oil runs out and there is only darkness.

Fred: Jesus knows how much darkness there is in this world. He wants you to have all you need to keep his light of faith burning.

Bill: And that is what these calls are about — not Jesus wanting to take up my time but to help me — to speak to me, to know me.

Fred: He knows how much you need him.

(Phone beeps)

Bill: *(Picks up the phone)* Maybe you are right — maybe it is time to answer this call.

2. The Prodigal Son

(Based on Luke 15:11-32)

Characters
    Sally
    Jane
    Son 1 (older son)
    Son 2 (younger son)
    Neighbor 1
    Neighbor 2
    Boss
    Father
    Slave

Sally: *(Talking to herself)* What's Jane up to now? Just sitting in her car. I suppose she's found some new sort of meditation.

(After a little while Jane gets up and moves to Sally)

Jane: Hi, Sally, sorry to keep you waiting.

Sally: Well, what were you doing?

Jane: Listening to the rest of the story. You know — Paul Harvey. He sure comes up with some good ones!

Sally: Here I thought you'd become some sort of mystic — and you were only listening to the radio. Well, let's get down to business. You and I have to come up with a Lenten service on the Prodigal Son. Any ideas?

Jane: We could have the confirmation class act it out. Anita is great with costumes.

Sally: That is a beginning. But what could we do to grab everyone's attention? Everyone knows the story so well already. We've got to do something different.

Jane: How about telling the rest of the story?

Sally: The rest of the story?

Jane: Yes, the story behind the story, like Paul Harvey does or like "Behind the Music" on VH1.

Sally: But with the Prodigal Son there isn't any story behind the story — there is just the story.

Jane: Maybe there is. How about this for an opening dialogue? The younger son is talking to his brother:

Son 2: The old man's got so much money — when he dies we'll be wealthy. Do you think it will be many years before he croaks?

Son 1: That's disgusting. How can you talk about our father in that way?

Son 2: I could be too old to enjoy it all. Maybe he lives to 95 — I'd be seventy — way too old for riding roller coasters and partying. Do you think there is some way we could speed this process up?

Son 1: Don't you have any respect for our father?

Son 2: I can't just say, "Drop dead, Dad." *(Pauses)* Or could I?

Son 1: What are you talking about?

Son 2: I think I will ask him to divide the inheritance now. He's such a softy, he'll go for it.

Sally: So you think that's the story behind the story? You make that younger son seem like a real jerk.

Jane: *(Pointing to Sally)* You got that one right! Can you imagine telling your father you want him to act as if he is dead so you can have your stuff now? This younger son is not a nice guy.

Sally: So where do you take the story from here?

Jane: I'd like to cut to the neighbors after he has done the dividing. They are talking about this father and his sons.

Sally: But there are no neighbors in Jesus' story.

Jane: Well, if there were, this is what they might be saying:

Neighbor 1: Did you hear about the shenanigans over at the Father-Had-Two-Sons household? That good for nothing younger son asked his dad to divide the inheritance and the old fool did! Just like that.

Neighbor 2: And that little twerp turned his half into cash and headed for the city.

Neighbor 1: Everyone is laughing. If my son even suggested such an idea, I'd disinherit him. But he said, "I'll be dead and you can have your money."

Neighbor 2: So what is he doing now that the two boys have everything?

Neighbor 1: His older son is supporting him. Though the father signed over all the property, the oldest son is acting as if the father is still in charge.

Neighbor 2: How can two such different boys come from the same family?

Neighbor 1: *(Shaking his head)* How could such a fool have such a fine son as that older boy?

Sally: That fits the story. Though no neighbors are mentioned by Jesus, someone is always watching.

Jane: And talking.

Sally: So what do you have planned for us next?

Jane: I think there is more to say about that moment before the younger son comes home.

Son 2: Oh, am I ever hungry! Hey, mister! Would it be all right if I ate some of these carob bean pods that I am shoveling for the pigs?

Boss: I didn't buy that feed for swine like you.

Son 2: *(As the boss walks away)* Jerk! *(Pauses)* My old man never treated anyone like this. *(Slight pause)* Say — I wonder what it would take to go to work for him? I'd have to make some kind of big apology. Let me think: Dad, I kind of messed up ... Oh, that won't do ... Hey, Pops, it wasn't my fault. I think the roulette wheel was rigged ... No, not that either. *(Thinks)* I could tell him someone mugged me and took all my money. *(Shakes his head)* He'd never believe it. I'll have to really crawl on the ground and grovel ... Father, I have sinned against heaven and before you and I am no longer worthy to be called your son ... Those are the right words. Then I hit on him for the job ... Yes, I'm no longer worthy to be your son; treat me like one of your hired servants.

Sally: I don't know. I think he was really sorry. I think he was sincere, not just making up a speech.

Jane: Well, it doesn't matter. Remember how the story went after that — how the father rushed out to meet him when he was still far away from home. And before he even spoke a word, the father was hugging him and kissing him.

Sally: But he gave his speech anyway — though he did leave out the part about being a servant.

Jane: He was all done bargaining. He finally understood that the father really loved him.

Sally: Now you have turned into the romantic. He didn't mention being servant because he thought: There is still a chance to be a son here! This guy is no good, through and through. Next week he'll be back to scheming again.

Jane: Is that why the older brother wouldn't join the party?

Sally: That and the fact that the calf the father slaughtered was part of the older brother's half of the inheritance. I can understand why that older brother was angry.

Jane: Yes, he was the responsible one. If he had done what his brother did, they all would have been starving.

Sally: He is just like the people at church who do all the work, who carry the burden.

Jane: So what is the rest of this story? That people never change?

Sally: And still the father rushes out to meet his no-good son.

Jane: Yet when the older brother won't join the party, the father goes out to meet him, too.

Sally: Maybe the rest of the story is God comes out to meet you and me wherever we are and hopes he can bring us all into the party that is his kingdom.

Jane: Hard workers and freeloaders alike.

Sally: Then the love of God is the beginning of the story and the end of the story and every story in between: this story, your story, my story.

Jane: Well, what do you think? Will we tell them the rest of the story this Lent?

Sally: No, let's just tell the story the way Jesus did.

(Jane and Sally move away from center stage where the parable will be acted out)

Sally: There was a man who had two sons. The younger of them said to his father:

Son 2: Father, give me the share of the property that will belong to me.

Sally: So he divided his property between them. A few days later the younger son gathered all he had and traveled to a distant country and there he squandered his property in dissolute living. When he had spent everything, a severe famine took place throughout that country, and he began to be in need. So he went and hired himself out to one of the citizens of that country, who sent him to his fields to feed the pigs. He would gladly have filled himself with the pods that the pigs were eating, and no one gave him anything. But when he came to himself he said:

Son 2: How many of my father's hired hands have bread enough and to spare, but here I am dying of hunger! I will get up and go to my father and I will say to him, "Father, I have sinned against heaven and before you; I am no longer worthy to be called your son; treat me like one of your hired hands."

Sally: So he set off and went to his father. But while he was still far off, his father saw him and was filled with compassion; he ran and put his arms around him and kissed him. Then the son said,

Son 2: Father, I have sinned against heaven and before you; I am no longer worthy to be called your son.

Sally: But the father said to the slaves:

Father: Quickly bring out a robe — the best one — and put it on him; put a ring on his finger and sandals on his feet. And get the fatted calf and kill it, and let us eat and celebrate for this son of mine was dead and is alive again; he was lost and is found!

Sally: And they began to celebrate. *(Pauses)* Now his elder son was in the field; and when he came and approached the house, he heard music and dancing. He called one of the slaves and asked what was going on. He replied:

Slave: Your brother has come and your father has killed the fatted calf, because he has got him back safe and sound.

Sally: Then the older brother became angry and refused to go in. His father came out and began to plead with him. But he answered his father:

Son 1: Listen: for all these years I have been working like a slave for you, and I have never disobeyed your command; yet you have never given me even a young goat so that I might celebrate with my friends. But when this son of yours came back who has devoured your property with prostitutes, you killed the fatted calf for him.

Father: Son, you are always with me and all that is mine is yours. But we had to celebrate and rejoice, because this brother of yours was dead and has come to life; he was lost and has been found.

3. The Good Samaritan

(Based on Luke 10:25-37)

Characters
    Fred
    Bill
    Lawyer
    Jesus
    Robbers (nonspeaking, two people)
    Priest (nonspeaking)
    Levite (nonspeaking)
    Samaritan (nonspeaking)
    Innkeeper (nonspeaking)

Fred: *(Stands near the altar watching Bill who is pacing from one side of the chancel to the other)* What do you think you are doing?

Bill: I am walking the road from Jerusalem to Jericho looking for someone to help.

Fred: And why are you doing that?

Bill: Jesus said to.

Fred: He did?

Bill: Remember the story he told about that Good Samaritan? How he found this guy all beat up and naked lying by the road — half dead — and how the Samaritan bandaged him and put him on his donkey and took him to an inn? Well, Jesus said, "Go and do likewise," so I am walking up and down the Jericho road looking for my chance. You think someone will get robbed and beat up soon?

Fred: *(Shakes head in disbelief)* I don't know.

Bill: I can see it now: Some guy really hurting and me coming to the rescue. Boy, I'd sure feel great then. Do you think I would make the evening news — maybe Channel 43? I just hope there is no blood. I hate the sight of blood.

Fred: *(Tries to break in)* Bill?

Bill: Somebody would probably call an ambulance — ruin the whole thing. They would come in with lights flashing and siren wailing and steal my moment of glory. It was sure easier to get eternal life back in Jesus' time.

Fred: Bill, I am kind of confused. What are you talking about?

Bill: I can tell you don't know your Bible. Let me refresh your memory. A lawyer stood up to put Jesus to the test. *(Motions to the choir loft where Jesus and the lawyer take over)*

Lawyer: Teacher, what must I do to inherit eternal life?

Jesus: What is written in the law? What do you read there?

Lawyer: You shall love the Lord your God with all your heart, and with all your soul, and with all your mind; and your neighbor as yourself.

Jesus: You have given the right answer. Do this and you shall live.

Bill: See, Fred, if you want to get eternal life, you have to love God with all your heart and soul and mind and love your neighbor as yourself.

Fred: I know that but what does this have to do with ambulances and the evening news?

Bill: Listen — you'll understand. You see, that lawyer wanting to justify himself, asked Jesus: "And who is my neighbor?" Jesus told this story:

(As Bill reads the parable — Luke 10:30-35 — Jesus takes the part of the man going down from Jerusalem to Jericho. When he falls after the Robbers have beaten him and robbed him and stripped him, Jesus falls with arms outstretched as if he is on the cross. The parable is acted out with Robbers, Priest, Levite, Samaritan, and Innkeeper all pantomiming their parts. Bill concludes with the line: "I will repay you for whatever more you spend.")

(Jesus takes his place once more with the lawyer)

Jesus: Which of these three, do you think, was a neighbor to the man who fell among robbers?

Lawyer: The one who showed him mercy.

Jesus: Go and do likewise.

Bill: Now do you get it? If I am going to get saved — I've got to do some saving. I sure hope the rescue squad doesn't get in the way.

Fred: I thought Jesus was the one who does the saving — not you.

Bill: Yes, I learned that in Sunday school but there's got to be more to it than just believing in Jesus. Maybe believing in him is a good beginning but then I need to do my part.

Fred: You are doing just fine, Bill.

Bill: No, I'm not. Everybody thinks I am a loser. I got passed over for a promotion last year — some young guy got the job I was hoping for. My wife never has the nice things the neighbor's wife has. My son is just like me — he works hard but just can't get ahead. If only I could save someone else — then I'd be a somebody.

Fred: You are probably right.

Bill: You're agreeing with me? You think I am a loser, too? Some friend you are.

Fred: We are all losers, Bill. Live your life however you want, but sooner or later you get to be the corpse on that road from Jerusalem to Jericho. And no Samaritan will come along to patch you up. Sooner or later you and I will have no clothes or money or life — and no spot on the evening news will save us then.

Bill: That's a depressing thought.

Fred: Not if you believe in Jesus. He took your place on that road — and mine. They stripped him, and beat him — robbed him of everything that he had. They made him the biggest loser of all. And so Jesus said, "I am having a party — only losers are invited. Only dead people get to be the life of this party."

Bill: Is this kind of like the last shall be first and the first last?

Fred: Or those who save their lives will lose them but those who lose their lives for my sake and the gospel's will save them.

Bill: So is that the part I get to play in this drama?

Fred: Truth is, Bill, you have been playing all the parts. And so have I.

Bill: Sometimes I am the one who does the hurting, the wounding, the injuring.

Fred: And sometimes I am the one so busy with my busyness that I rush right by someone who needs a friend to stop, to listen, to help.

Bill: Sometimes I do see the injured one. I care. I stop. I help.

Fred: Sometimes I have been like the innkeeper — helping through my work. I get paid but I am helping just the same.

Bill: And so many times I have been the injured one.

Fred: And others have taken time.

Bill: Loved me as they have loved themselves.

Fred: I am thankful for them and for Jesus.

Bill: They haven't walked by.

Fred: And when you are the biggest loser of all in death, Jesus won't walk by either. He will take you to where his Father is the innkeeper. He has already paid for your care.

Bill: Well, I'd still like to help someone. It makes me feel good.

Fred: I hope you can. I hope we all can help someone.

4. The Rich Man

(Based on Mark 10:17-27)

Characters
  Fred
  Bill
  Chorus 1
  Rich Man
  Chorus 2
  Jesus
  Disciples
  Parents (nonspeaking)
  Children (nonspeaking)

Fred: Hi, Bill, how ya doin?

Bill: Pretty good. You?

Fred: Okay. Though I must say I have been doing a lot better ever since I read the newsletter from my old church. At last someone has taken action.

Bill: About what?

Fred: Hymns — hymns that no one can sing.

Bill: You mean like the one we sang a few weeks ago?

Fred: Exactly. But at my old church the council has taken action. They went through the hymnal and made a list of forbidden hymns. Never again will they have to suffer through verse after verse of torture.

Bill: It might be worth running for council just to do that here.

Fred: And while we were at it there is something else we could do. We could make a list of passages that the preachers need to preach on at least once a year.

Bill: Yes, it seems like some Bible stories never get read. Like my favorite, "The Little Engine That Could."

Fred: "The Little Engine That Could"?

Bill: Yes, the story about the engine that is pulling a long load of cars and when he comes to the mountain can't make it to the top. But then he learns to say, "I think I can, I think I can, I think I can," and the next thing you know he has made it. Our pastors should preach on that — a good positive message instead of so much negativity.

Fred: "The Little Engine That Could" is a children's story. It is not in the Bible.

Bill: Well, it should be. We could paste it in over that one we heard a few weeks ago — what a depressing story that was.

Fred: Which one was that?

Bill: You know, about the rich man who came to Jesus.

Fred: The one Jesus loved who went away sad?

Bill: Yes, he wanted to be saved. Jesus should have told him the story of The Little Engine That Could. His story would have had a happy ending.

Fred: Do you remember how the story started? Let me read it to you from Mark's Gospel but in the style of "The Little Engine That Could." I'll pick some lines that will be repeated all the way through — kind of like the "I think I can, I think I can," but with different words.

(Jesus, the Disciples, the Parents, and Children enter and act out what Fred reads)

Fred: People were bringing little children to Jesus that he might touch them and the disciples spoke sternly to them. But when Jesus saw this he was indignant and said to them:

Jesus: Let the little children come to me; do not stop them, for it is to such as these that the kingdom of God belongs. Truly I tell you, whoever does not receive the kingdom of God as a little child will never enter it.

Chorus 1: Whoever does not receive the kingdom of God as a little child receives it will never enter it.

(Jesus stands, the Children and Parents leave and the Disciples and Jesus begin walking)

Chorus 1: Whoever does not receive the kingdom of God as a little child receives it will never enter it.

Fred: As Jesus was setting out on a journey, a man ran up *(Rich Man acts this out)* and knelt before Jesus and asked him:

Rich Man: Good teacher, what must I do to inherit eternal life?

Jesus: Why do you call me good? No one is good but God alone.

Chorus 2: No one is good except God alone.

Jesus: You know the commandments: You shall not murder ...

Chorus 2: No one is good except God alone.

Jesus: You shall not commit adultery, you shall not steal ...

Chorus 2: No one is good except God alone.

Jesus: You shall not bear false witness. You shall not defraud. Honor your father and mother.

Rich Man: Teacher, I have kept all of these since my youth.

Chorus 2: No one is good except God alone.

Chorus 1: Whoever does not receive the kingdom of God as a little child receives it will never enter it.

Fred: Jesus looking at him loved him and said:

Jesus: You lack one thing. Go sell what you own and give the money to the poor and you will have treasure in heaven. Then come, follow me.

Fred: When he heard this he went away grieving, for he had many possessions.

(Rich Man exits; Jesus and Disciples remain)

Chorus 2: No one is good except God alone.

Chorus 1: Whoever does not receive the kingdom of God as a little child receives it will never enter it.

Bill: See what I mean. What a depressing story — even Jesus' love for that man could not save him. And even if he had given all his stuff away, I don't think that would have saved him either. No one is good enough to inherit eternal life. That was your point, wasn't it?

Fred: Well, not exactly. When that man had left, Jesus looked around and said to his disciples:

Jesus: How hard it will be for those who have wealth to enter the kingdom of God.

Chorus 1: Whoever does not receive the kingdom of God as a little child receives it will never enter it.

(Disciples look perplexed)

Jesus: *Children*, how hard it is to enter the kingdom of God. It is easier for a camel to go through the eye of a needle than for someone who is rich to enter the kingdom of God.

Disciples: Then who can be saved?

Jesus: For mortals it is impossible, but not for God. For God all things are possible.

Bill: So what is the point?

Fred: I think that rich people, successful people, going to church people, backbone of the community people have all learned your story well. They know how to say, "I think I can, I think I can, I think I can."

Bill: And Jesus wants us to learn to chant a new chant instead?

Fred: I think God can, I think God can, I think God can. The impossible has happened, something bigger than squeezing a camel through the eye of a needle. God's Son has given his life for all the Little Engines That Can't.

Bill: Even for preachers who pick unsingable hymns?

Fred: And rich young men who can't let go of their wealth.

Bill: Now that's good news!

5. The Great Banquet

(Based on Luke 14:16-24)

Characters
  Fred
  Bill
  Slave
  First One
  Second One
  Third One
  Owner

Fred: Where are you going with those tools, Bill?

Bill: I'm heading to the church to do some pew chopping.

Fred: Pew chopping?

Bill: Pew chopping. The pastor said that the pews are too big, that we have too many. I thought I'd go over to the church and fix the problem.

Fred: I don't get it. I would think it is a good thing if we have room for lots of people at church.

Bill: No, it's a bad thing. The church is always half empty — it gets depressing. When I'm done it will always look like we have a crowd. Everyone will feel great.

Fred: I thought that the goal was to bring more people in, not to reduce the seating to fit the crowd.

Bill: That's the old way of thinking. That fits with sending missionaries to Africa and New Guinea — or bringing the neighbor's children to church. Back then Jesus was for them, but now Jesus is just for us.

Fred: For us?

Bill: People who are just like us — our families and our friends, people in our neighborhood.

Fred: I don't think that is the way Jesus sees things. Remember his advice? "When you give a luncheon or dinner do not invite your friends or your brothers, or your relatives or rich neighbors, in case they may invite you in return, and you would be repaid. But when you give a banquet, invite the poor, the crippled, the lame, and the blind because they cannot repay you."

Bill: Who wants to go to a church full of people like that — full of needy people? I sure don't. By the time Sunday comes I need a lift. I'm sure not looking to do any more lifting.

Fred: But what about what Jesus said?

Bill: Jesus said lots of things — some of which I like — and a lot I don't pay much attention to. I guess this stuff about inviting the poor, the lame, the crippled, and the blind goes with the latter.

Fred: Well, I'm sure of one thing — Jesus is not in the business of reducing the seating. Remember the parable he told?

Bill: Which one?

Fred: The one about the great dinner. Someone gave a great dinner and invited many. At the time for the dinner, he sent his slave to say to those who had been invited:

Slave: *(Goes to First One who is sitting in congregation on aisle)* Come, for everything is ready now.

First One: I have bought a piece of land, and I must go out and see it; please accept my regrets. *(Exits to the rear of the sanctuary)*

Slave: *(Goes to Second One who is sitting in congregation on aisle)* Come, for everything is ready now.

Second One: I have bought a yoke of oxen, and I am going to try them out; please accept my regrets. *(Exits to the rear of the sanctuary)*

Slave: *(Goes to Third One who is sitting in congregation on aisle)* Come, for everything is ready now.

Third One: I have just been married, and therefore I cannot come. *(Exits to the rear of the sanctuary)*

Fred: So the slave returned to his master. Then the owner of the house became angry and said to his slave:

Owner: Go out at once into the streets and lanes of the town and bring in the poor, the crippled, the blind, and the lame.

(Slave goes out into congregation and gathers people for the banquet table[s].)

Slave: Sir, what you ordered has been done and there is still room.

Owner: Go out, then, into the roads and lanes, and compel people to come in, so that my house may be filled. For I tell you none of those who were invited will taste my dinner.

(Slave gathers enough to fill the tables)

Bill: I don't like that story. Jesus makes it sound like the church is for the leftovers — the losers. It sounds like the only reason there is a place for us is because the in-crowd didn't come.

Fred: Maybe that is true. Have you ever noticed how some people just don't have time to help out around the church or to pound some nails at Habitat? Or how they don't take time to get to know the little ones at church?

Bill: What do you mean?

Fred: Do you notice how some people would just rather give their money than themselves?

Bill: That may be but I don't think that is what this parable is about.

Fred: Then what do you think it is about?

Bill: I think it is about who we belong to — who we belong with. God's people are the ones who bring only their need to the dinner. God's people are the hungry people.

Fred: Well, there aren't many hungry people in this neighborhood. We would have to buy a bus in order to fill the church with hungry people.

Bill: I'm not so sure. I think everybody on my street is pretty hungry when it comes to some things. I look at the faces I see — so many of them are sad.

Fred: But what am I going to do — knock on their front doors and say, "You sure look sad, how would you like to come to my church and fill the pews?"

Bill: Maybe, but in a different way. You don't need to knock on the door. You could take time for a conversation when you are out pulling some weeds. Take time to ask questions — to take a real interest.

Fred: I'm too busy for that.

Bill: Busy with what? Going to inspect the new field you have bought — or the oxen — busy because you reserve all your time and energy for your wife and your children?

Fred: Could be.

Bill: It is not God we have no time for — but our hungry neighbors.

Fred: And that is why there are too many pews. But I know one thing for sure — if we will not fill these pews with people, God won't let God's dinner go to waste.

Bill: You mean that if we won't go out and bring people to God's feast, someone else will?

Fred: The church down the street?

Bill: Or in Africa or South America.

Fred: God will find someone to share the feast he has prepared — if not us and our children, then someone else's.

Bill: Even the poor, the crippled, the blind, and the lame.

Fred: Even them. *(Pauses as Bill goes toward the pew and gets out his saw)* What are you doing?

Bill: I'm going to cut up the pews. We've got too many. The pastor said so.

Fred: But I thought we had just decided that God wants these pews filled?

Bill: Maybe not these. *(To congregation)* What do you think? Cut them up or fill them up? Know any hungry ones you could bring?